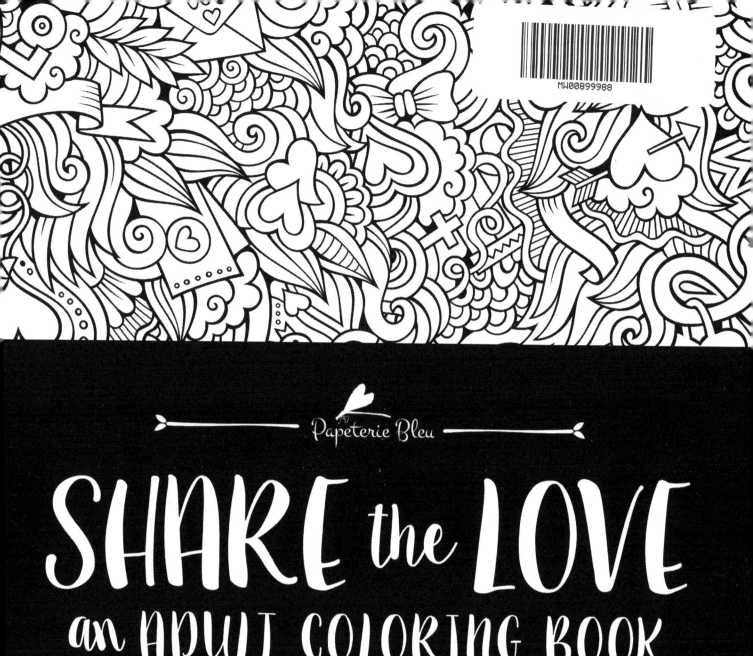

Papeterie Bleu

SHARE the LOVE
an ADULT COLORING BOOK

ISBN-13: 978-1530281862

ISBN-10: 1530281865

FREE DOWNLOAD

www.papeteriebleu.com/stleng

YOUR DOWNLOAD CODE: STL7695

 @papeteriebleu

 Papeterie Bleu

 Papeterie Bleu

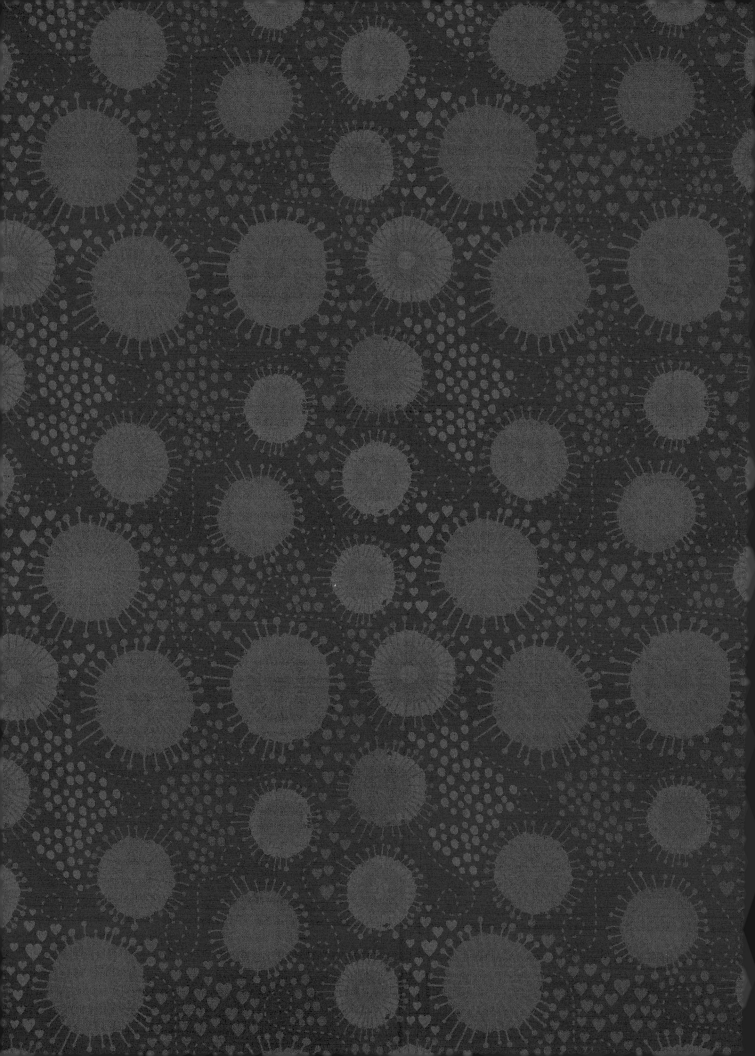

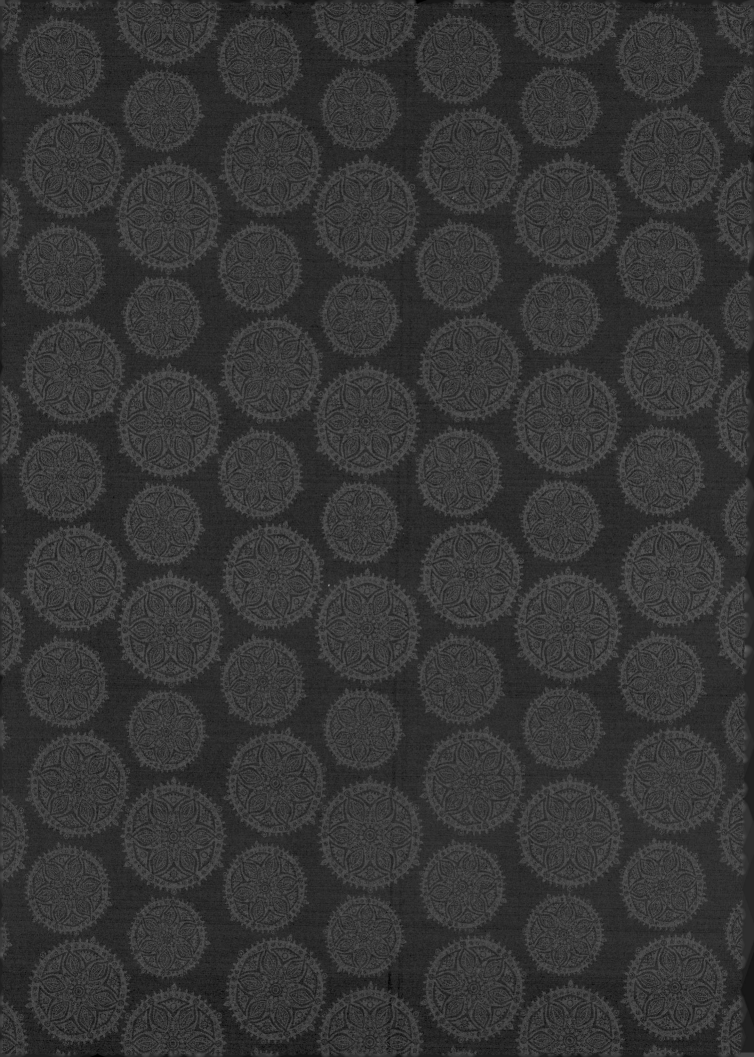

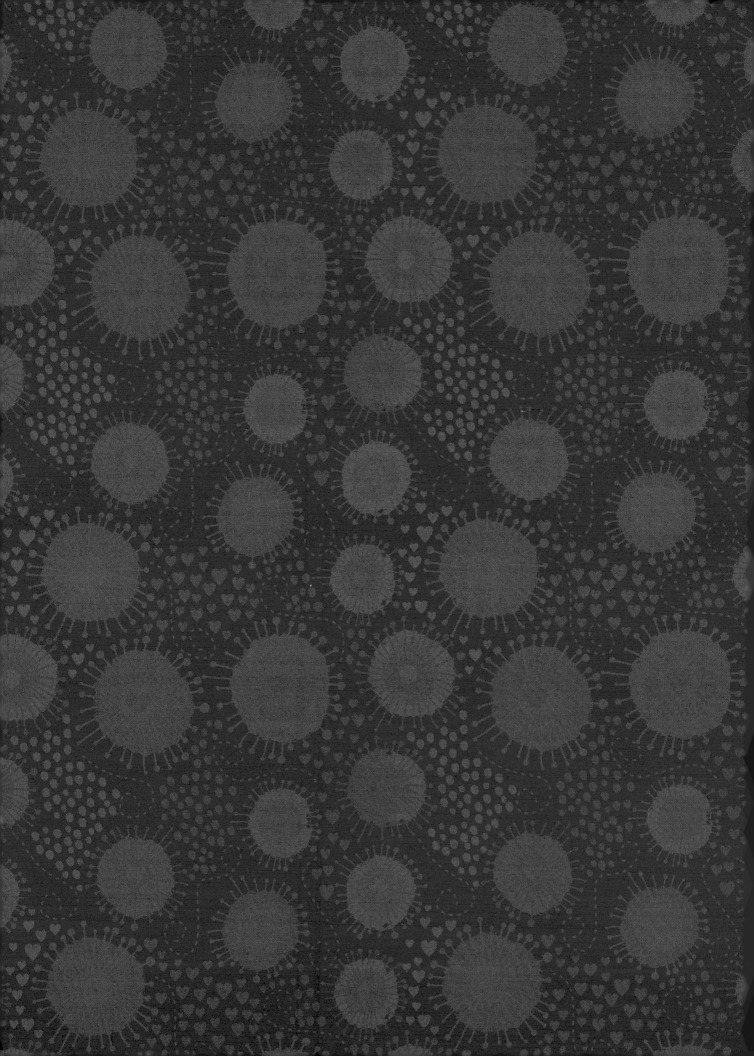

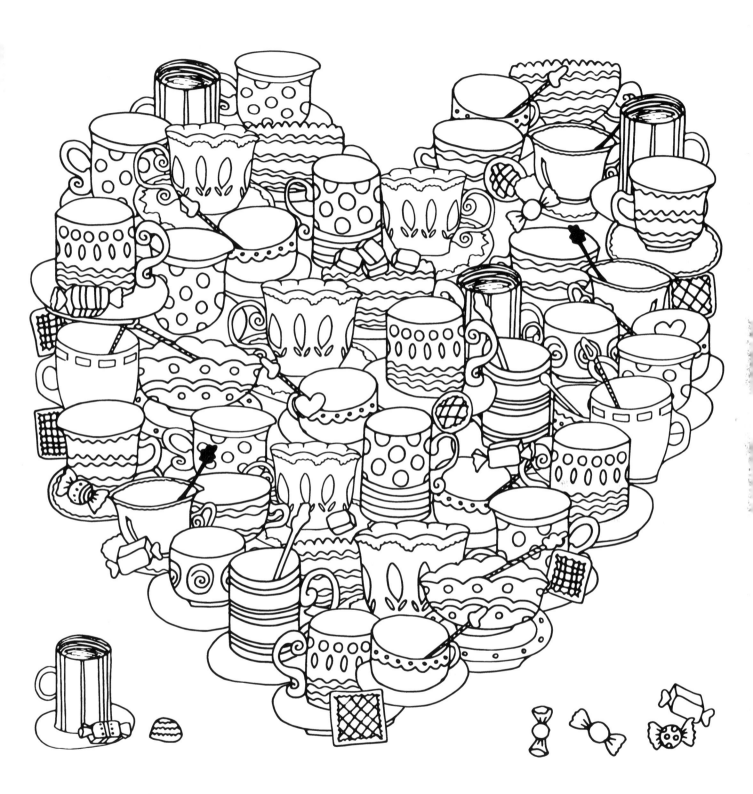

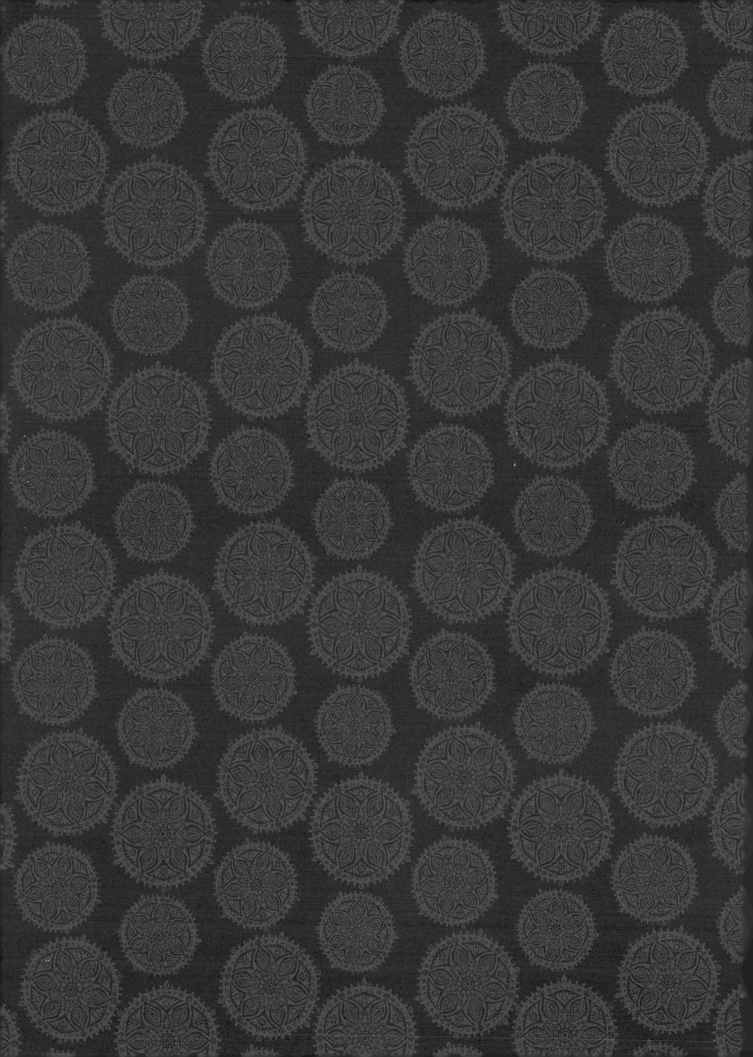

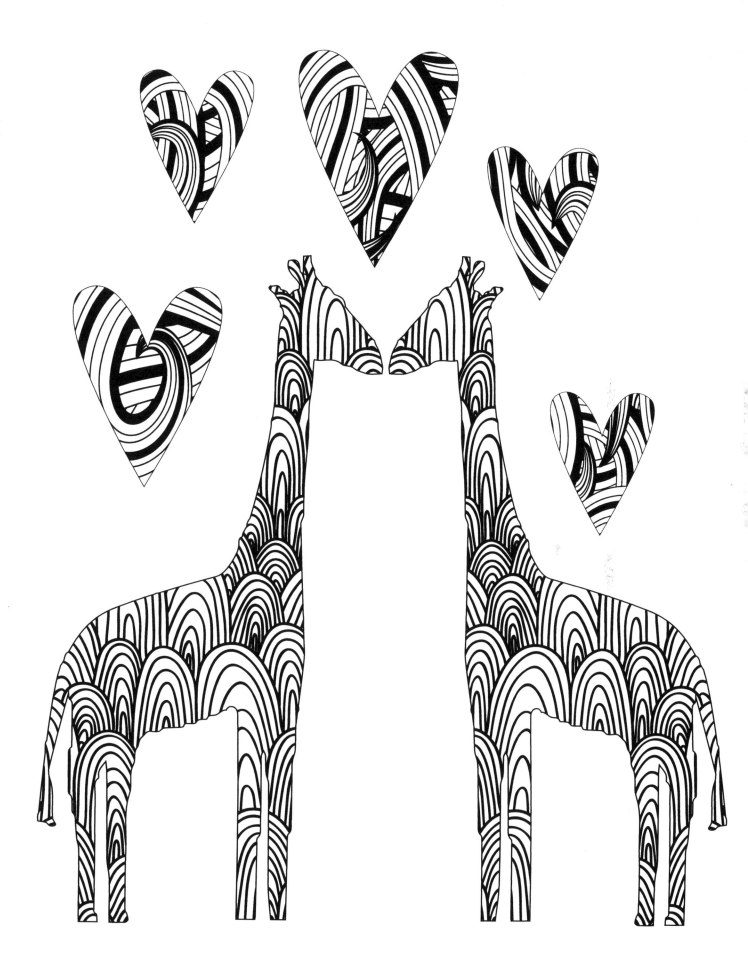

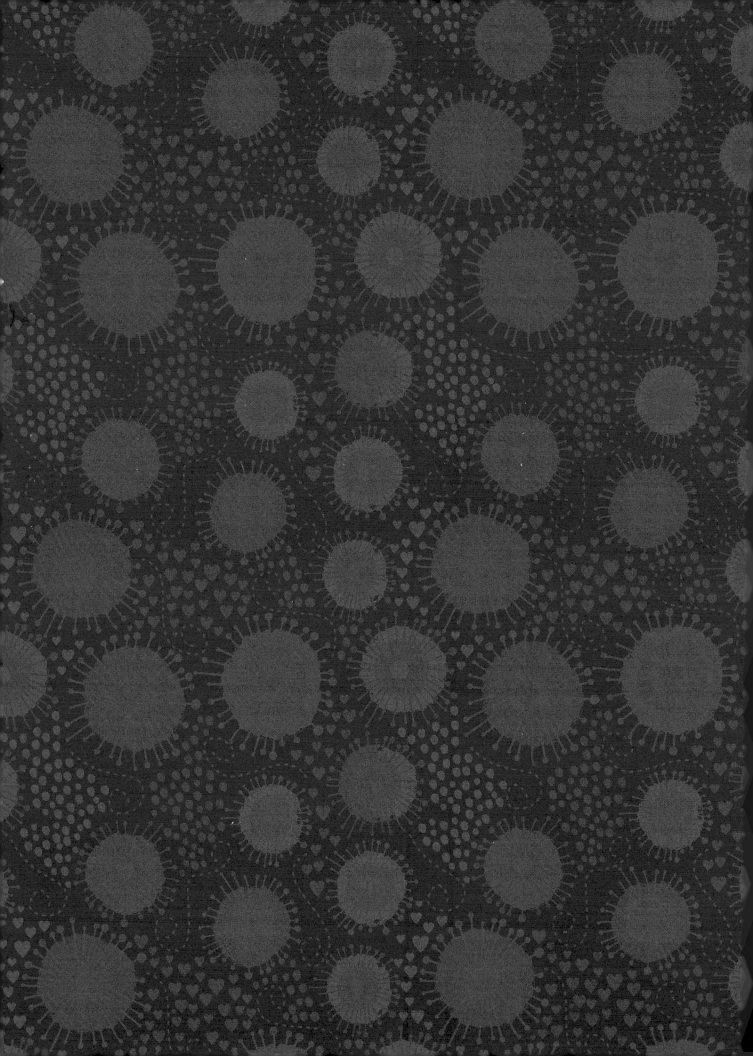

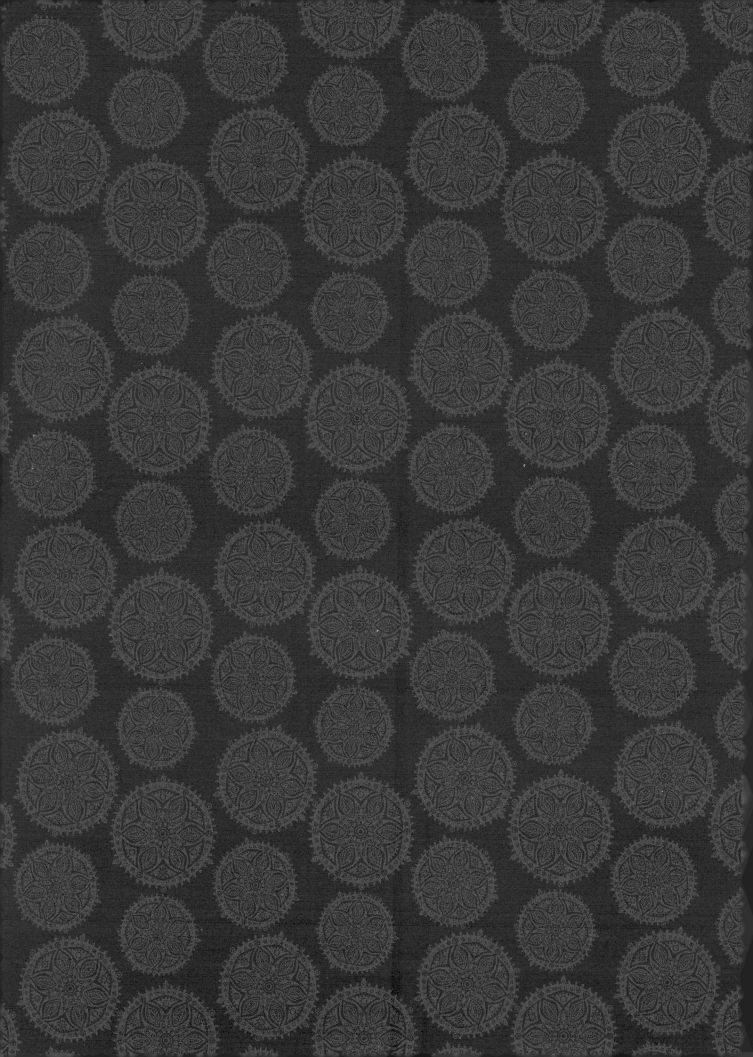

BE SURE TO FOLLOW US ON SOCIAL MEDIA FOR THE LATEST NEWS, SNEAK PEEKS, & GIVEAWAYS

[Instagram] @PapeterieBleu

[Facebook] Papeterie Bleu

[Twitter] @PapeterieBleu

ADD YOURSELF TO OUR MONTHLY NEWSLETTER FOR FREE DIGITAL DOWNLOADS AND DISCOUNT CODES

www.papeteriebleu.com/newsletter

CHECK OUT OUR OTHER BOOKS!

www.papeteriebleu.com

    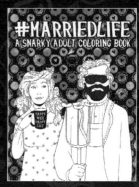

CHECK OUT OUR OTHER BOOKS!

www.papeteriebleu.com

Sugar SKULLS at MIDNIGHT
an ADULT COLORING BOOK

SUGAR SKULLS at MIDNIGHT VOLUME 2
ANIMALS & ALIENS ADULT COLORING BOOK

DÍA DE LOS MUERTOS
MIDNIGHT Edition
SUGAR SKULL COLORING BOOK

DÍA DE LOS PERROS
MIDNIGHT Edition
DOG SUGAR SKULL COLORING BOOK

MANDALAS at MIDNIGHT
an ADULT COLORING BOOK

EVERYONE IS THE WORST
MORE MANDALAS?!? UGH.
MIDNIGHT EDITION
A SNARKY MANDALA COLORING BOOK

UGH. I CAN'T EVEN.
MANDALAS? MEH.
MIDNIGHT EDITION
A SNARKY MANDALA COLORING BOOK

HATERS GONNA HATE
MANDALAS? AGAIN?!? SMH.
MIDNIGHT Edition
A SNARKY MANDALA COLORING BOOK

WONDERLAND at MIDNIGHT

WONDERLAND at MIDNIGHT 2
A FANTASY ADULT COLORING BOOK

well BLESS your HEART!
A CHALKBOARD COLORING BOOK
SOUTHERN SAYINS' & SASS

SHARE the LOVE
an ADULT COLORING BOOK

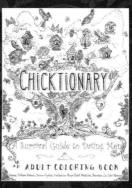

CHICKTIONARY
A Survival Guide to Dating Men
an ADULT COLORING BOOK

CHECK OUT OUR OTHER BOOKS!

www.papeteriebleu.com

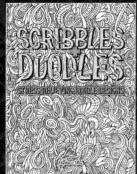

Made in the USA
Middletown, DE
20 April 2018